Module 4

The Mighty Word:
Building Vocabulary and Oral Language

LETRS

Language Essentials
for Teachers of
Reading and
Spelling

Louisa C. Moats, Ed.D.

SOPRIS WEST EDUCATIONAL SERVICES
A CAMBIUM LEARNING COMPANY

BOSTON • NEW YORK • LONGMONT, CO

08   6 5

Proofread by Susan Defosset
Cover design and text layout by Sue Campbell
Slide design by Christine Kosmicki
Production assistance by Sherri Rowe and Kim Harris

ISBN 1-59318-192-2

Printed in the United States of America

Published and Distributed by

SOPRIS
WEST
EDUCATIONAL SERVICES

4093 Specialty Place • Longmont, CO 80504 • (303) 651-2829
www.sopriswest.com

Dedication

To my husband, Steve Mitchell, whose support is constant and invaluable.

Acknowledgments

The LETRS modules have been developed with the help of many people. Our active national trainers, including Carol Tolman, Susan Hall, Marcia Davidson, Anne Cunningham, Marcia Berger, Deb Glaser, Linda Farrell, Judi Dodson, and Anne Whitney have all offered valuable suggestions for improving the module content and structure. Their devotion to delivering LETRS across the country is appreciated beyond measure. Bruce Rosow, Kevin Feldman, Susan Lowell, Patricia Mathes, Marianne Steverson, Lynn Kuhn, Jan Hasbrouck, and Nancy Eberhardt contributed their expertise to the first edition and continue to provide essential input and feedback. Many other professionals from all over the country who have attended institutes and offered constructive criticism have enabled our response to educators. I hope you see your ideas reflected in the revised editions of this continually evolving material.

I am grateful for the daily support and energy of the Sopris West office staff, editors, and designers including Lynne Stair, Sue Campbell, Sandra Knauke, Christine Kosmicki, and Kim Harris. Special thanks are due to Toni Backstrom, who manages the LETRS program with enthusiasm, competence, and commitment.

Stu Horsfall, Ray Beck, Steve Mitchell, Chet Foraker, and Steve Kukic are the vision and energy behind the publication of evidence-based programs in education that will help all children learn. I am so fortunate to be working with all of you.

—LCM

Contents for Module 4

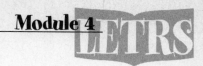
Overview of LETRS: Language Essentials for Teachers of Reading and Spelling

LETRS is designed to enrich and extend, but not to replace, program-specific professional development for teachers of reading and language arts. Teachers who implement a core, comprehensive reading program must know the format and instructional routines necessary to implement daily lessons. Teaching reading is complex and demanding, and new teachers will need both modeling and classroom coaching to implement the program well. Program-specific training, however, is not enough to enable teachers to tailor instruction to the diverse needs in their classrooms. Even teachers who are getting good results will need to understand the research-based principles of reading development, reading differences, and reading instruction. Reaching *all* learners through assessment and intervention is only possible when the teacher understands who is having difficulty, why they might be struggling, and what approaches to intervention are grounded in evidence. An empowered teacher is one who knows and can implement the best practices of the field, as established by a scientific research consensus.

The American Federation of Teachers' *Teaching Reading Is Rocket Science* and the Learning First Alliance's *Every Child Reading: A Professional Development Guide* provided the blueprint for these modules. LETRS modules teach concepts about language structure, reading development, reading difficulty, and assessment practices that guide research-based instruction. The format of instruction in LETRS allows for deep learning and reflection beyond the brief "once over" treatment the topics are typically given. Our professional development approach has been successful with diverse groups of teachers: regular classroom and special education, novice and expert, rural and urban.

The modules address each component of reading instruction in depth—phonological and phonemic awareness; phonics, decoding, spelling, and word study; oral language development; vocabulary; reading fluency; comprehension; and writing—as well as the links among these components. The characteristics and the needs of second language learners (ELL), dialect speakers, and students with other learning differences are woven into the modules. Assessment modules teach a problem-solving strategy for grouping children and designing instruction.

Teachers usually need extended time to learn and apply the knowledge and skills included in LETRS, depending on their background and experience. The content is dense by design. Each module is written so that teacher participants will engage in questions, problems, and tasks that lead to understanding, but understanding may occur in small steps, gradually, over several years. Some of the modules also are accompanied by the LETRS Interactive CD-ROMS, self-instructional supplements for independent study and practice, developed with the help of a grant from

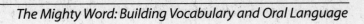
the SBIR program of the National Institute for Child Health and Human Development.

More information about LETRS material, programs, and institutes is available at www.letrs.com.

Content of LETRS Modules Within the Language-Literacy Connection

Components of Comprehensive Reading Instruction	Organization of Language						
	Phonology	Morphology	Orthography	Semantics	Syntax	Discourse and Pragmatics	Etymology
Phonological Awareness	2	2					
Phonics, Spelling, and Word Study	3, 7	3, 7, 10	3, 7, 10				3, 10
Fluency	5		5	5	5		
Vocabulary	4	4	4	4	4		4
Text Comprehension		6		6	6	6, 11	
Written Expression			9, 11	9, 11	9, 11	9, 11	
Assessment	8, 12	8, 12	8, 12	8, 12	8, 12	8, 12	

Objectives

◆ Understand the many facets of word meaning

◆ Appreciate the role of vocabulary knowledge in reading comprehension

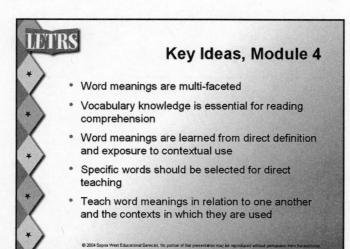

Key Ideas, Module 4

- Word meanings are multi-faceted
- Vocabulary knowledge is essential for reading comprehension
- Word meanings are learned from direct definition and exposure to contextual use
- Specific words should be selected for direct teaching
- Teach word meanings in relation to one another and the contexts in which they are used

♦ Identify the ways in which word meanings are learned, in oral and written language

♦ Experiment with the role of context in word learning

♦ Develop a rationale for choosing specific words for direct instruction

♦ Generate multiple meanings for words and understand why instruction of multiple meanings and multiple uses is important

♦ Practice semantic feature analysis to appreciate how words are related in meaning

♦ Practice categorizing and understand its importance

♦ Sketch a lesson plan for teaching vocabulary in or related to a specific text

What does it mean to know a word? Module 4 begins an inquiry into this question. We consider that words are known in relation to one another, that word knowledge has many facets, and that vocabulary growth can be indirectly and directly influenced. Other modules have addressed the organization of language at the levels of sounds, symbols, meaningful word parts (morphemes), sentences, and discourse, but this one is all about words.

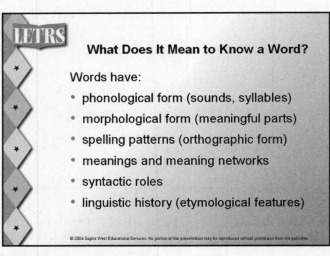

What Does It Mean to Know a Word?

Words have:
• phonological form (sounds, syllables)
• morphological form (meaningful parts)
• spelling patterns (orthographic form)
• meanings and meaning networks
• syntactic roles
• linguistic history (etymological features)

© 2004 Sopris West Educational Services. No portion of this presentation may be reproduced without permission from the publisher.

Slide 4

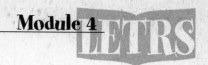
Vocabulary and Learning to Read

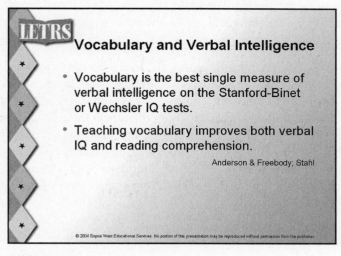

LETRS
Comprehension Depends on Knowing Word Meanings

* Vocabulary knowledge is strongly related to overall reading comprehension.

* If a word is decoded and pronounced but the meaning is not recognized, comprehension will be impaired.

* Knowledge of a word's meaning also facilitates accurate word recognition.

  The phonological, orthographic, and meaning processors all contribute to reading!

© 2004 Sopris West Educational Services. No portion of this presentation may be reproduced without permission from the publisher.

Slide 5

Knowledge of word meanings is a major contributor to text comprehension. The National Reading Panel (2000) confirmed that the depth and breadth of a learner's vocabulary contributes substantially to proficient reading. Consequently, explicit and implicit exploration of word meanings should occur often during reading instruction.

LETRS
Vocabulary and Verbal Intelligence

* Vocabulary is the best single measure of verbal intelligence on the Stanford-Binet or Wechsler IQ tests.

* Teaching vocabulary improves both verbal IQ and reading comprehension.

Anderson & Freebody; Stahl

© 2004 Sopris West Educational Services. No portion of this presentation may be reproduced without permission from the publisher.

Slide 6

Getting at the meaning of a written passage requires knowledge of the individual words in the passages. Vocabulary tests predict and are highly correlated with general reading comprehension tests. Vocabulary also correlates very highly with the overall verbal reasoning quotients of IQ or

cognitive ability tests. If psychologists need to estimate the verbal abilities of a student, using one quick measure, they often use a vocabulary test. Vocabulary is said to be a proxy or stand-in for verbal reasoning ability.

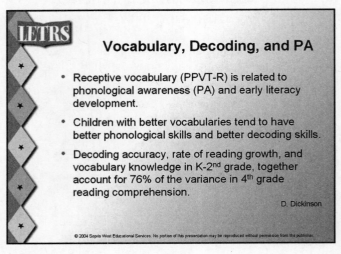

Slide 7

If children do not know the meanings of words they are decoding, they may pronounce them but not understand the gist of the passage or how phrases go together. Recognition of a new word in print is easier and faster if the word already has an identity (a pronunciation and meaning) in the mind of the reader. The child who is a good decoder nevertheless must identify the meaning and use of a word in a specific context in order to comprehend.

Children who are learning English (ELL) or who have limited language development will require intensive, deliberate instruction in word meanings in addition to phonics and word recognition. Children learning English may be more adept at decoding than they are at interpreting what they read. The size of the child's vocabulary in his or her first language will affect how readily he or she learns the vocabulary of a second language. Word learning in the first language and overall language proficiency in ELL children is related to the ease with which they learn English.

Defining "Vocabulary"

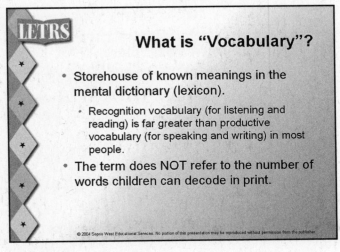

Slide 8

The term **vocabulary** refers to the storehouse of word meanings that we draw on to comprehend what is said to us, express our thoughts, or interpret what we read. The **lexicon** is the mental dictionary, the storage file of the **meaning processor**. The meaning processor makes sense of word parts, phrases, sentences, illustrations, and punctuation marks. Meaning also resides in the context surrounding specific words; otherwise, we would not be able to pronounce and interpret word forms such as *object* (n.) and *object* (v.). In other sources, the word "vocabulary" is sometimes used to refer to the words that students can pronounce or recognize in print. That is a misuse of the term, as students may pronounce words they see in print without knowing their meanings.

Size of Young Readers' Listening and Reading Vocabularies

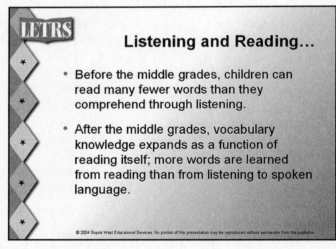

A Grown Vocabulary: What Do Children Need to Learn ?

- Nagy and Anderson (1984) estimated that there are 88,700 word families in text up to 12th grade.
- 107 words account for 50% of the words in running text.
- 5,000 more words account for an additional 45% of the words in running text.
- Infrequent words (5% of total) carry the most unique meaning in a passage.

© 2004 Sopris West Educational Services. No portion of this presentation may be reproduced without permission from the publisher.

Slide 9

Listening and Reading…

- Before the middle grades, children can read many fewer words than they comprehend through listening.

- After the middle grades, vocabulary knowledge expands as a function of reading itself; more words are learned from reading than from listening to spoken language.

© 2004 Sopris West Educational Services. No portion of this presentation may be reproduced without permission from the publisher.

Slide 10

When children begin formal reading instruction at the end of kindergarten or beginning of first grade, their listening vocabulary is far greater than their reading vocabulary. By third or fourth grade, normally progressing children begin to encounter more words in print than they already know for listening and speaking. At that point, growth in vocabulary depends more and more on reading itself and the ability to derive meanings of new words as they are encountered in context. Let's consider why that is the case.

How Do Children Learn the Words They Know?

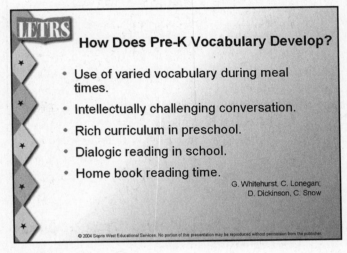

Slide 11

Learning of word meanings occurs rapidly from birth through adolescence within communicative relationships. Everyday experiences with friends, care-givers, and community members shape speech habits and knowledge of language. The human mind latches onto new words as it hears them because the words are the tools of communication. Humans have an intrinsic need to understand what is said to them and to share experience through language, and the brain is biologically adapted to support language acquisition. Before school and before learning to read, children learn most of the words they know through daily oral language with adults. Adults facilitate that process when they introduce new words in a shared experience, elaborate what a child has said, confirm and clarify the child's attempts to use new words, deliberately repeat new words in conversation, or read aloud.

Great differences exist, however, in the exposure to language of children with highly verbal or nonverbal parents. Imagine the verbal styles of three mothers taking their children to the grocery store.[1]

---

[1] The author is indebted to Phyllis Hunter, reading consultant from Texas, for her dramatization of these styles at a Reading First meeting.

Mother #1 (low verbal). [Child in the grocery cart.] Sit still. [Child reaching toward the avocado]. Keep your hands to yourself.

Mother #2 (average). [Child in grocery cart.] What should we have for dinner? See anything good, honey? We haven't had carrots for a while. [Child reaching toward the avocado.] Put that back, now.

Mother #3 (high verbal). [Child in grocery cart.] Oh, what do we see here? Organic avocado? Do you know what "organic" means, sweetie? It's when the farmer says she doesn't put any pesticides on the plants. What's a pesticide? It's something that kills pests. Pests are insects that eat up the green leaves on the top of the plant. The plant needs the green leaves for all that green chlorophyll that goes into that yummy green mushy stuff we make guacamole with. Guacamole? That's a Spanish word!" [Child says, "Mommy, you talk too much!"]

Exercise #1: How We Learn Words

Think of a word you have learned recently. What was the context for that learning? What motivated you to learn and remember that word?

_____

_____

_____

_____

_____

Exercise #1, Examine Word Learning

Vocabulary development continues throughout life, although at a much slower rate after formal education ends.

• What word have you learned lately?

• In what context?

• Through what means?

• What motivated you?

Slide 12

How Many Words Do Children Know on School Entry?

Highly verbal adults may enrich their children's vocabularies continually. But children whose chief exposure is to nonverbal adults or adults who do not engage them in reading or conversation have many fewer opportunities to learn new words. Hart and Risley's (1995) study of verbal-linguistic adult behavior in households with high socioeconomic (SES) and low SES parents documented that low SES children are exposed to one-third of the verbiage that children from high SES, highly verbal families are exposed to. By the time they enter school, low SES children may know one-half or fewer of the word meanings known by typical middle class children, and far fewer than more privileged children. Once that gap is established, it is very difficult to make up. Normally progressing children who already have an advantage in word knowledge are continuing to learn words at a faster rate than less verbal children. This widening gap is what Stanovich referred to as the "Matthew Effect," whereby the verbally rich get richer and verbally poor get poorer.

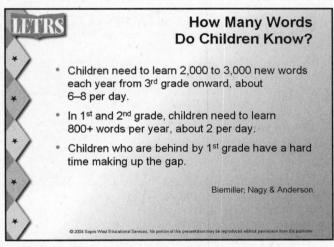

Slide 13

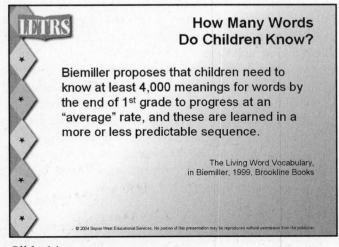

Slide 14

Andrew Biemiller, who has studied the number of words children typically know by each age and grade level, estimates that by third grade, advanced children's word knowledge is equivalent to that of average children in fourth grade (Biemiller, 1999, p. 1). Slower children, at about the 25th percentile in third grade, are similar to average second graders. Less verbal children begin school knowing perhaps 1,000 root words and 2,000 meanings for those words, but an average child knows roughly 2,000 words and 4,000 meanings for those root words in first grade.[2] To make up this "language gap," as it is called by Hirsch (2001), the less verbal child would have to learn vocabulary at a considerably faster rate than his average classmates. The average child increases his or her knowledge of root words to about 8,000 by sixth grade, but verbally limited children may have learned about 4,000 in the same time span.

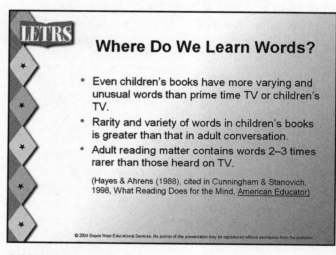

Slide 15

What role do books play in preschool word learning? The Hayes and Ahrens study from 1989, reported again in Cunningham and Stanovich's (1998) essay, "What Reading Does for the Mind," documents that well-written children's books are richer in unusual vocabulary than typical adult conversation, peer conversation, or typical television programs. Books embody more uncommon and content-rich words than any other verbal medium, right from the beginning. Thus, word learning requires exposure to the language of books. Furthermore, the language of books is most attainable when adults pause while reading and engage children in conversations about new words and concepts and relate those concepts to their own experience. As children learn to read themselves, reading begets verbal growth; new words can be deciphered more easily from context as vocabulary and verbal fluency increase, and more new words are encountered when text exposure is high.

---

2 Biemiller's vocabulary list of root words known by most children by grade 4 is listed in the appendix of *Language and Reading Success* (1999).

What Does "Knowing a Word" Mean?

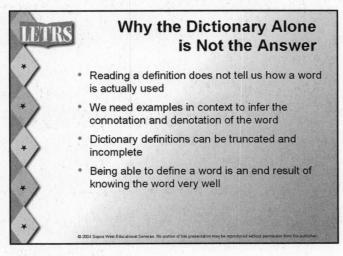

Slide 16

Words are learned through both indirect and direct processes. The mind indirectly constructs the meaning of words that are encountered in various contexts. Beck et al. (2002) have estimated that children typically need 10 to 12 exposures to words used in multiple contexts in order to learn their meanings indirectly. During that process of acquiring and consolidating a word's meaning, children are unsure and groping for evidence to confirm their idea of the word. Partial knowledge of a word is a sample of an incomplete and unelaborated entry into the mental dictionary. Students also learn a smaller number of words from direct teaching or from being given a definition from someone else. Direct teaching of vocabulary succeeds when it deepens and enriches knowledge of word meanings and when it emphasizes the relationships among words and concepts. Good instruction often does not begin with a definition; rather, the ability to give a definition is often the result of knowing what the word means.

The dictionary has been described as a repository for aging words, a historical record of words' origins and evolutions. We cannot learn to speak from memorizing the dictionary. Definitions do not tell us how a word is used. "Precious" is defined as "having great value" and being "costly" in Webster's New World dictionary. A child learning "precious" from a definition is likely to misuse the word ("His leather jacket was precious") unless its use and connotation are demonstrated.

Shallow and Deep Word Knowledge

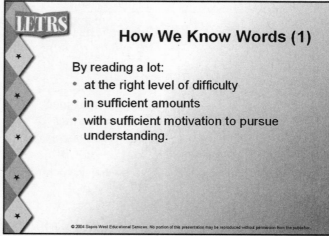

Slide 17

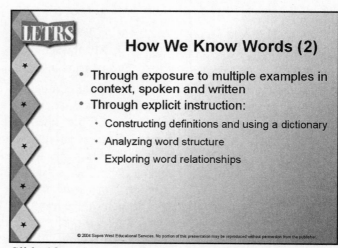

Slide 18

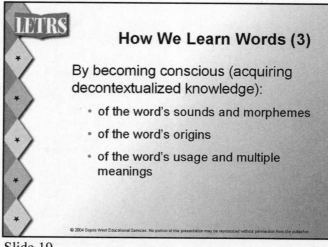

Slide 19

Learning what a word means necessitates multiple experiences with the various uses and meanings of the word. Children (and adults) commonly have partial or shallow knowledge of a word, sometimes because the word has only been encountered in a limited context. For example, from watching an older sibling come home with a friend's belonging, children might think that the word "borrowed" means "given" without an understanding that something borrowed must be returned. The word "designated" might mean "sober" to a child who has only heard the phrase, "designated driver." The word "job" might mean only what the child's parent does, not the whole category of various jobs. A grasp of deep meaning is signified when multiple meanings and uses are understood, when the word can be used with precision in writing or speech, and when a definition can be generated. The ability to define a word is a *result* of word knowledge.

Exercise #2: Exploring the Use of Words in Context

Work with a partner. Choose an important word that is specific to a hobby or area of special knowledge that you have—a "jargon" word that a layperson would not know. Make up several sentences that use the word. Can your partner figure out what the word means? Could he or she define the word on the basis of the contextual uses you gave? How close was the meaning your partner came up with? What are the advantages and limitations of context use in word definition?

_____

_____

_____

_____

_____

LETRS

Exercise #2, Meaning from Context

Explore what it is like to give and derive the meaning of a new word from context alone.

- Pick a specialty word from your vocabulary.
- Create a sentence or two for your partner designed to convey the word's meaning from context.
- See if your partner can define the word you illustrated.

Example: <u>Joists</u> that held up the laths prevented us from remodeling the space with a cathedral ceiling. [parallel beams that hold up a ceiling or floor]

Slide 20

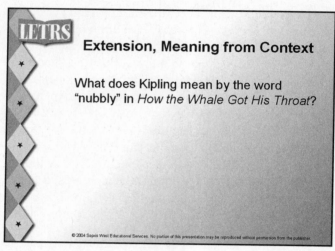

Slide 21

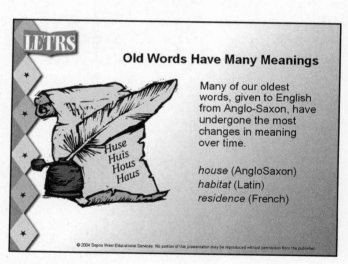

Slide 22

Words have connotations and denotations that determine how they may be used in specific contexts, and many have more than one meaning. Our oldest, most common words seem to have developed the most varied meanings over time (see Appendix A). Looking at the Oxford English Dictionary, for example, one can see that the word "house" has dozens of definitions and that it entered our lexicon from Anglo-Saxon. Its first uses were noted in Beowulf in the 800's A.D. The word "residence," however, entered our language from Norman French about 500 years later, was used by Chaucer in the 1300's, and has only a few meanings.

Exercise #3: Multiple Meanings

How many meanings and uses can you think of for the following common words: frame, check, pitch. Take one word and list all the meanings you know without using a dictionary. Then, check the dictionary for others you may have missed.

_____

_____

_____

_____

_____

_____

_____

_____

_____

LETRS

Exercise #3, Multiple Meanings

Pick a common word and list as many meanings and uses for the word as you can within 5 minutes.

frame

check

pitch

© 2004 Sopris West Educational Services. No portion of this presentation may be reproduced without permission from the publisher.

Slide 23

LETRS

Extension, Multiple Meanings

* Are there any words in _How the Whale Got His Throat_ that have several meanings that could be explained during vocabulary study?

© 2004 Sopris West Educational Services. No portion of this presentation may be reproduced without permission from the publisher.

Slide 24

The construction of meaning around a word is also individual and personal. Two of us might interpret the word "republican" very differently depending on our prior experience, beliefs, and acculturation. The sense we have of our own understanding or misunderstanding is **metacognition**. Comprehension depends upon knowing when and what we have not comprehended, for example recognizing when our understanding of a word may diverge considerably from understandings shared by others. If we are adaptive and willing to search for more information, we can readily adjust our internal definition of a word.

Our knowledge of words, or lexical knowledge, is organized in networks of meaning. Thus, we are able to remember and recall words that are associated with the same topic more quickly than we can recall words that have no meaningful connection. Those meanings are often organized in hierarchical networks; that is, we spontaneously categorize or group ideas together and recognize categories that have intrinsic similarities. In turn, the reality of meaning networks and categories can be exploited in purposeful teaching. Words and concepts should be learned in relation to one another and in relation to a topic of interest, not as isolated units. New words are remembered and retrieved more easily if they are filed in a meaning network whose structure is familiar. Effective teaching will:

♦ elaborate various connections among better known and less-well known words,

♦ deepen and enrich existing knowledge, and

♦ build a network of ideas around key concepts that are well elaborated.

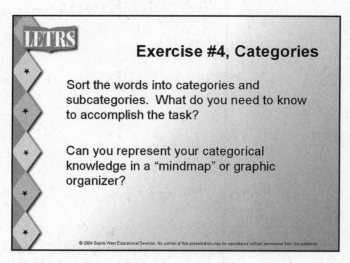

Exercise #4, Categories

Sort the words into categories and subcategories. What do you need to know to accomplish the task?

Can you represent your categorical knowledge in a "mindmap" or graphic organizer?

Slide 25

Exercise #4: Categories

Put the following words on cards and then sort them into categories and subcategories. What do you need to know to accomplish this task?

mushing	Bruno	bones	fur/hair
jobs	Lassie	sniffing	retriever
kibbles	greyhound	famous dogs	legs
dogs	Rin-Tin-Tin	leading	spaniel
milkbone	tail	food	Fido
searching	terrier	breeds	body parts

Which graphic organizer in Appendix B would be most suitable for showing these word relationships?

LETRS

Exercise #5, Making Definitions

- A <u>darkroom</u> is a <u>room for developing photographs</u> that has <u>very dim, special light and running water</u>.

- To <u>plunder</u> is to <u>rob or pillage</u>, usually <u>by an invading or conquering group.</u>

© 2004 Sopris West Educational Services. No portion of this presentation may be reproduced without permission from the publisher.

Slide 26

More on definitions. Dictionary definitions often follow a formal structure. They denote the category to which something belongs, provide a synonym, and then elaborate the concept's distinguishing features or properties. For example, *granola* is a *breakfast cereal* of *rolled oats*, *wheat germ*, and *other grains*, that is considered a *healthy "whole food."*

As children learn vocabulary, their incomplete knowledge of a word may be reflected in their ability to give only part of a definition. For example, if asked to define "lake," they may say "it has lots of water." A goal of instruction is to give them a complete and elaborated definition.

© The New Yorker Collection 1998 by Tom Cheney. Reprinted with permission.

"It all depends on how you define 'chop.'"

Exercise #5: Structure of Definitions

Use the following format to make a definition for each word below.

A _____ is (a) _____ that (is, does) _____.

(critical features)

Words to define:

River: _____

_____

_____

_____

_____

_____

Phoneme: _____

_____

_____

_____

_____

_____

Bison: _____

_____

_____

_____

_____

_____

Semantic feature analysis. The critical or defining features of words are sometimes formally presented or analyzed in charts that show the contrast between two similar or overlapping concepts. Content words (nouns, verbs, adverbs, adjectives) have many attributes known as **semantic properties**. The better a word is known, the more of its properties or features are known. Words that overlap extensively in meaning qualify as **synonyms**. Words that overlap very little and have opposite connotations qualify as **antonyms**. Many words have semantic overlap but are not synonyms for one another.

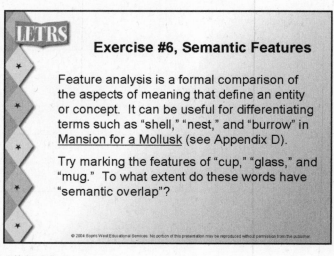

LETRS

Exercise #6, Semantic Features

Feature analysis is a formal comparison of the aspects of meaning that define an entity or concept. It can be useful for differentiating terms such as "shell," "nest," and "burrow" in <u>Mansion for a Mollusk</u> (see Appendix D).

Try marking the features of "cup," "glass," and "mug." To what extent do these words have "semantic overlap"?

Slide 27

"A billion is a thousand million?
Why wasn't I informed of this?"

Exercise #6: Semantic Feature Analysis

If the object at the top of a column has the feature designated on the left, mark a (+).
If the object does not have the feature, mark a (–). How extensively do these meanings
overlap? Are the words synonyms or not?

	OBJECTS		
FEATURES	**cup**	**glass**	**mug**
Have a handle			
Made from clay			
Made from glass			
Round shape			
Taller than round			
For hot liquid			
For cold liquid			
Made from paper			
Used for wine			

Exercise #7: How Groups of Words Are Alike

In what way are the following groups of nouns the same and a little different?
In what ways do their semantic features overlap?

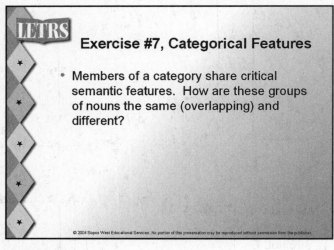

Slide 28

1. daughter, sister, niece   vs.   nun, waitress, actress
    _____

2. rooster, bull, ram   vs.   hen, ewe, cow
    _____

3. table, chair, pencil   vs.   water, cream, sand
    _____

4. table, chair, pencil   vs.   faith, hope, charity
    _____

5. husband, brother, son   vs.   clerk, preacher, judge
    _____

6. grandfather, mother, nephew   vs   brother, sister, cousin
    _____

Semantic Features

- Some nouns are countable:
    carrots, dollars, tables, windows
- Some nouns are not countable:
    rice, water, glass, steel, dirt
- Some verbs require an object, others don't:
    slept, dozed, thought
    gave, promised, borrowed

© 2004 Sopris West Educational Services. No portion of this presentation may be reproduced without permission from the publisher.

Slide 29

Other kinds of semantic features. Words also have other properties or features that determine how they can be used in sentences and what words we combine with them or substitute for them. For example, nouns may be subdivided into those that are **countable** and those that are not. Countable nouns take the quantifier adjectives *many* and *few*; non-countable or mass nouns take the adjectives *much* and *less*. You can eat *too many carrots* but not *too much carrots*, or *too much rice* but not *too many rices*. You can have *too few dollars* or *less money* than you'd like. The word *more* can modify either type of noun.

Verbs may be subdivided into those that must take a direct object and those that can stand alone without an object. Verbs are "marked" as needing other words to go with them. The **transitive property** of a verb means it requires an object. For example, I can *subject* someone to something but I can't *subject* (with no object). I can *reject* someone for something but I can't just *reject*. On the other hand, I can *procrastinate* all by myself, without doing anything to anyone but me. Other intransitive verbs are *sleep*, *think*, and *hesitate*. *Sleep* and *think* can be followed by prepositional phrases (*I will sleep* until *9:30. I thought* about *what you said...*). But the word *hesitate* is usually followed by an infinitive (*I hesitated* to call *you...*). Content words, including nouns and verbs, contain grammatical properties that most speakers of the language know just by hearing the words spoken often in context.

Tip for Teaching

Teaching a word's meaning may necessitate explaining its part of speech and showing how it must be used in a sentence.

Antonyms and Scaling

- Gradable antonyms: tiny -----enormous
- Complementary antonyms:
  black------white, dead-------alive
- Gradable antonyms lend themselves to scaling of terms to show degrees of an attribute.

putrid foul stinky unpleasant scented fragrant intoxicating

© 2004 Sopris West Educational Services. No portion of this presentation may be reproduced without permission from the publisher.

Slide 30

Types of opposites. Antonyms are words of opposite meaning, but there are two important subtypes to consider: **gradable** or **complementary** antonyms. **Gradable antonyms** take meaning from the context in which they are used. Their meaning is relative and expresses the degree to which an attribute characterizes a person or object. For example to say that one house is "enormous" and the other is "tiny" does not convey any fixed amount of space occupied by either house. The words refer to points on a continuum that vary according to one's perspective on houses. Gradable antonyms lend themselves to the activity of **scaling** or putting words on a continuum to express degrees of meaning. *Enormous, huge, large, average, small, tiny,* and *miniscule* convey a scale of size. Scaling is a verbal exercise that can help a writer be more precise in word choice and help young readers refine their knowledge of word meanings.

Complementary pairs of opposites are dichotomous and do not represent points on a scale. The qualities exist in a complementary relationship; if one condition exists, the other cannot, and vice versa. There are no gradations between the opposite conditions. One can be married or single; dead or alive; male or female. The expression, *he sees things in black and white* means, he thinks that if something is one thing it cannot be the other. This type of person thinks of opposites as complementary when in fact they are gradable; there is a continuum of qualities between the points on a continuum that we refer to as the "gray."

A common way of forming antonyms in the language is to add prefixes including *un, in, non, mis,* or *dis* to words as permitted: *happy/unhappy; hospitable/inhospitable; conformist/nonconformist; identify/misidentify; allow/disallow.*

Exercise #8: Antonym Pairs and Scaling

Check the antonym pairs as complementary (either/or) or gradable (opposite ends of a continuous scale).

	Complementary	Gradable
dead – alive		
hot – cold		
above – below		
fat – skinny		
married – single		
fragrant – putrid		
angry – delighted		
hideous – gorgeous		
straight – bent		
honest – devious		
winner – loser		

Now take one of the *gradable* antonym pairs and fill out the scale from one extreme to the other with words that show degrees of meaning.

Figure 4.1: Dimensions of Word Knowledge

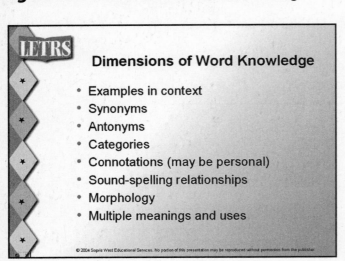

Slide 31

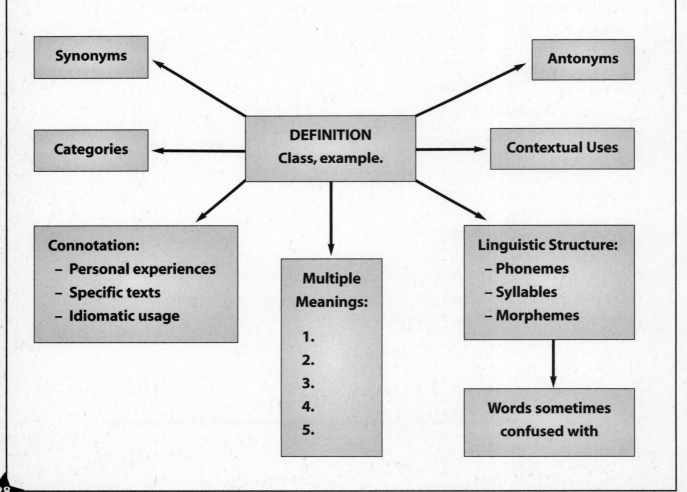

Teaching Vocabulary

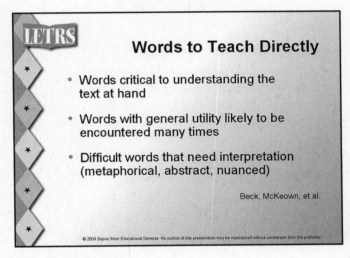

Slide 32

Which Words Should Be Directly Taught?

a. *Words important to the theme of a passage read* and discussed in the classroom should be chosen and emphasized first. Those words may or may not be in the written text that the children are reading. For example, in Chapter 9 of *Stuart Little*, Stuart the mouse finds himself in a dumpster covered with wet, smelly garbage. The scene invites a discussion of words for smells, even a scaling of words from *putrid* to *fragrant*, even though they are not used in the text.

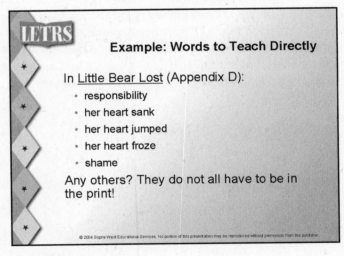

Slide 33

b. *Words that are useful and likely to be encountered again* soon can be revisited in other contexts. For example, words for human emotions and relationships will be useful whenever characters in narratives are discussed. *Guilt*, *gratitude*, *indebtedness*, *greed*, and *wisdom* are useful words.

c. *Difficult words that need interpretation*, such as figures of speech, idioms, or words that refer to background information that is central to understanding the text must be tackled directly. More time should be spent elaborating their meanings. For example, if a passage is about animal habitats, the concept of habitat and words describing habitats should be directly presented.

Which Words Can Be Explained Briefly?

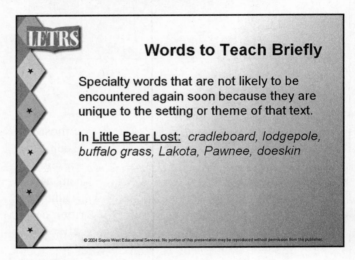

Slide 34

Children's texts often include specialty words needed to understand the topic at hand that will not be encountered again soon. Those words can be sorted out and explained briefly before reading and during reading itself. Elaborate exercises or memorization are not worthwhile for words with a limited range of use. For example, if the story is about a weaver, terms such as *shuttle* or *spindle* might be used but they do not require instructional focus.

Provide Multiple Examples of Word Use in Varied Contexts

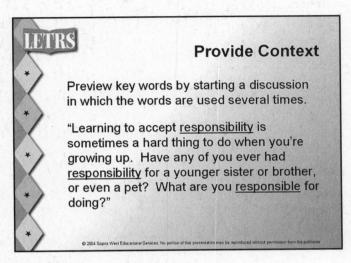

Provide Context

Preview key words by starting a discussion in which the words are used several times.

"Learning to accept <u>responsibility</u> is sometimes a hard thing to do when you're growing up. Have any of you ever had <u>responsibility</u> for a younger sister or brother, or even a pet? What are you <u>responsible</u> for doing?"

© 2004 Sopris West Educational Services. No portion of this presentation may be reproduced without permission from the publisher.

Slide 35

Especially before reading a new selection, preview the most important vocabulary by using the words in spoken sentences and seeing if the students can begin to form an idea of their meaning. Hearing the words spoken and used is essential; if students do not hear them used in their classroom, they may never be exposed. Many published reading programs begin lessons with a list of new words with which a written definition is to be matched. That exercise may be more worthwhile after the children have heard the teacher use the words several times.

Teach the Relationship Between Word Structure and Word Meaning

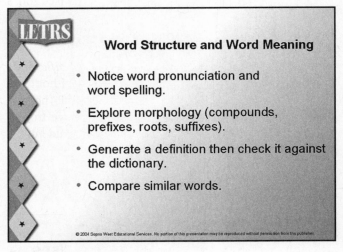

Slide 36

Meaningful parts of words—compounds, inflectional endings, prefixes, suffixes, roots and base words—connect words with other known words. Recognition of meaningful parts can help students figure out meanings of new words encountered in context, and can help them organize their mental dictionary for easy access to words in memory. For example, a second or third grader will benefit from knowing that *misery* and *miserable* are related and from thinking about why the word *miser* shares meaning with *misery*.

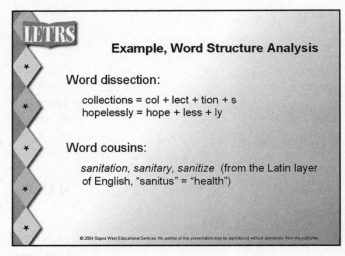

Slide 37

The Mighty Word: Building Vocabulary and Oral Language

A third grader can learn that the words *bisect*, *dissect*, *intersect*, *insect*, and *section* share a root (meaning to *cut*). They can be asked what each of these words has to do with the idea of cutting or segmentation. They could be asked to speculate on the meaning of "sector" or "trisection."

Be Sure the Students Can Pronounce the Word

Students confuse similar sounding words such as *pacific* and *specific*, *then* and *than*, *shocked* and *shot*, *bisect* and *bicept*. Without an accurate and complete phonological representation of a word (how it is pronounced, with all sounds enunciated) students will have trouble sorting out the meaning. Check pronunciation; always have students pronounce new words accurately.

Teach Multiple Meanings and Uses

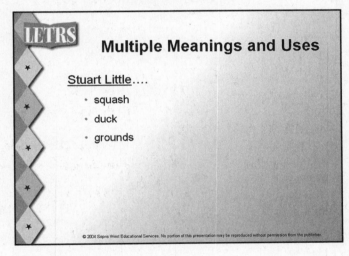

Slide 38

Even the words first encountered in decodable text often have multiple meanings. Students who learn new uses and meanings for known words develop more flexibility and curiosity about words, or greater word consciousness. For example, if the students read "jam," they should be able to think of both a traffic jam and the jam spread on toast. They are also likely to expect other words they know to have new meanings.

Teach Idioms, Metaphors, and Colloquial Uses of Language

Students who are learning English as a second language, who are concrete or literal in their interpretation of language, or who have not been exposed to wide ranging uses of words and phrases, may be stymied by the metaphoric nature of verbal expression. "She's gone to the dogs." "He ran out of luck." "Let's kill some time before the game." "She's taken nothing from nobody."

© The New Yorker Collection 2001 Gahan Wilson. Reprinted with permission.

*"You're supposed to push your envelope
from the <u>inside</u>, Conners!"*

Use Graphic Organizers to Show How Words Are Related

Especially after reading a passage, word webs and graphic organizers that depict categories and comparisons are very helpful for defining and deepening word knowledge. Word webs and graphic organizers from the *LANGUAGE!* curriculum (Sopris West) provide good examples of the formats that can be devised and are included in Appendix B.

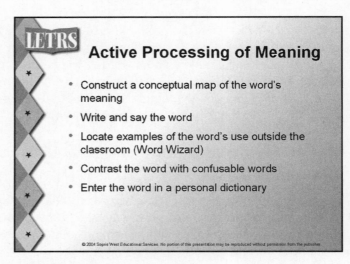

Active Processing of Meaning

- Construct a conceptual map of the word's meaning
- Write and say the word
- Locate examples of the word's use outside the classroom (Word Wizard)
- Contrast the word with confusable words
- Enter the word in a personal dictionary

© 2004 Sopris West Educational Services. No portion of this presentation may be reproduced without permission from the publisher.

Slide 39

Exercise #9, Plan Instruction

Select one or more of the narrative or expository texts provided at the end of the module.

With a small group, decide on the words that are most important to teach directly and thoroughly (5–10). List words that might be taught more briefly as well.

Outline a few activities that would be useful for building vocabulary before, during, or after reading the selection.

© 2004 Sopris West Educational Services. No portion of this presentation may be reproduced without permission from the publisher.

Slide 40

Exercise #9: Apply Strategies to Teaching Text

Focusing on one or more texts in Appendix C, work with a small group to a) select the words that you would teach directly and b) devise strategies for teaching those words. Indicate whether you are likely to use the strategies before reading, during reading, or after reading.

Summary

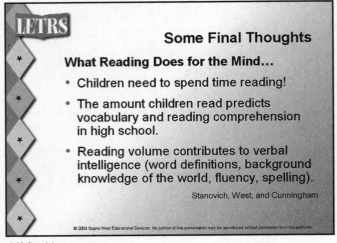

Slide 41

Understanding what we read depends not only on the ability to decode the words in print but also to know their meanings. Comprehension is highly dependent on knowledge of word meanings. Knowledge of a word is learned gradually after multiple exposures to words in speech and print. Students can be encouraged to learn new words by piecing together meanings from context, word parts (morphemes), and dictionary definitions. Many word meanings are learned indirectly from exposure. Thus, there is no better way to build vocabulary than through reading itself.

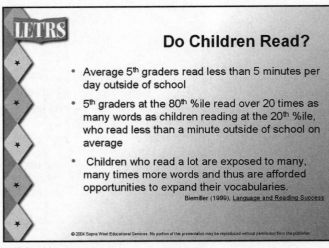

Slide 42

Direct vocabulary instruction targets specific vocabulary that is a) very useful, b) central to the meaning of that passage, or c) difficult to figure out independently. Between 10 and 15 new words a week are usually targeted for direct teaching. Relationships among words should be emphasized. Synonyms, categories, antonyms, overlapping meanings, thematic associations, analogies, class-example relationships, and figures of speech all can be employed in the discussion of word meanings and their associations.

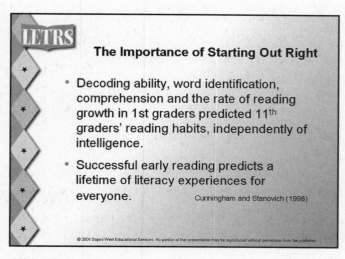

Slide 43

The dictionary is an indispensable reference, but dictionary definitions are often incomplete, misleading, or useless for knowing how to use a word. We don't "own" new words until we have been exposed to them, investigated them, and used them appropriately ourselves. Knowledge of word meanings is necessary for proficient reading and writing, and, paradoxically, those meanings will be learned most readily from reading itself and from a stimulating linguistic environment. Teachers' verbal behavior in the classroom is pivotal in providing students the exposure, the models, and the incentives they need to pursue word learning.

Finally, remember these principles:

◆ Motivate students to read or listen to challenging text.

◆ Prioritize critical high utility vocabulary for direct teaching.

◆ Actively engage students in "deep processing"—integrating and applying new words across contexts.

◆ Don't waste time memorizing definitions or telling children to use words in sentences if they do not yet understand them.

Instructional Resources for Vocabulary

Dictionaries

Longman Dictionary of American English

The Basic Newbury House Dictionary of American English

Merriam-Webster Online: www.m-w.com

Software

www.inspiration.com

Masterminds@graphicorganizers.com

Power Vocabulary: www.lexile.com

Bibliography

Anderson, R. C., & Freebody, P. (1983). Vocabulary knowledge. In H. Singer and R. Ruddell (Eds.), *Theoretical models and processes of reading*, 3rd Edition, 343–371. Newark, DE: International Reading Association.

Beck, I. L., McKeown, M. G., & Kucan, L. (2002). *Bringing words to life: Robust vocabulary instruction.* New York: Guilford Press.

Biemiller, A. (1999). Language and reading success. In J. Chall (Ed.), *From reading research to practice, A series for teachers.* Cambridge, MA: Brookline Books.

Carlisle, J., & Rice, M. S. (2003). *Reading comprehension: Research-based principles and practices.* Baltimore: York Press.

Chall, J. S., Jacobs, V. A., & Baldwin, L. E. (1990). *The reading crisis: Why poor children fall behind.* Cambridge, MA: Harvard University Press.

Cunningham, A. E., & Stanovich, K. E. (1997). Early reading acquisition and its relation to reading experience and ability ten years later. *Developmental Psychology, 33*, 934–945.

Cunningham, A. E., & Stanovich, K. E. (1998). What reading does for the mind. *American Educator, 22*, 8–15.

Dickinson, D. K., & Smith, M. W. (1994). Long-term effects of preschool teachers' book readings on low-income children's vocabulary and story comprehension. *Reading Research Quarterly, 29*, 104–123.

Dickinson, D. K., & Snow, C. E. (1987). Interrelationships among prereading and oral language skills in kinder-garteners from two social classes. *Early Childhood Research Quarterly, 2*, 1–25.

Flavell, R., & Flavell, L. (1995). *Dictionary of Word Origins.* London: Kyle Cathie Limited.

Hart, B., & Risley, T. R. (1995). *Meaningful differences in the everyday experience of young American children.* Baltimore: Paul Brookes.

Hirsch, E. D. (2001). Overcoming the language gap. *American Educator, 25* (2), 4, 6–7.

Irvin, J. L. (1997). *Reading the middle school student* (2nd Ed.). Boston: Allyn and Bacon.

Kacirk, J. (2000). *The word museum: The most remarkable English words ever forgotten.* New York: Touchstone.

Nagy, W., & Anderson, R. C. (1984). The number of words in printed school English. *Reading Research Quarterly, 19*, 304–30.

RAND Reading Study Group. (2002). *Reading for understanding: Toward an R & D program in reading comprehension.* Washington, DC: Office of Education Research and Improvement.

Sable, P. (2001). Vocabulary: Teaching words and their meanings. In S. Brody (Ed.), *Teaching reading: language, letters, and thought.* (pp. 254–275). Milford, NH: LARC Publishing.

Stahl, S. A. (1999). *Vocabulary development.* In J. Chall (Ed.), From *Reading research to practice*, A series for teachers. Cambridge, MA: Brookline Books.

Stanovich, K. E., West, R. F., & Cunningham, A. E. (1991). Beyond phonological processes: Print exposure and orthographic processing. In S. Brady & D. Shankweiler (Eds.), *Phonological processes in literacy* (pp. 219–235). Hillsdale, NJ: Erlbaum.

Sternberg, R. J. (1987). Most vocabulary is learned from context. In M. G. McKeown & M. E. Curtis (Eds.), *The nature of vocabulary acquisition* (pp. 89–106). Hillsdale, NJ: Erlbaum.

Whitehurst, G. J., & Lonigan, C. J. (2001). Emergent literacy: Development from prereaders to readers. In S. B. Neumann and D. K. Dickinson (Eds.), *Handbook of early literacy research* (pp. 11–29). New York: Guilford Press.

Glossary

affix: a morpheme or meaningful part of a word attached before or after a root to modify its meaning; a category that subsumes prefixes, suffixes, and infixes

Anglo-Saxon: Old English, a Germanic language spoken in Britain before the invasion of the Norman French in 1066

automaticity: performance without conscious effort or attention; a characteristic of skill mastery

base word: a free morpheme to which affixes can be added, usually of Anglo-Saxon origin

cognitive desktop: a figurative expression referring to the working memory capacity of the mind and the available attentional resources in consciousness

colloquialism: an expression used in informal speech

complementary antonyms: words that are categorical and dichotomous (either/or) opposites, such as *dead* or *alive*

concept: an idea that links other facts, words, and ideas together into a coherent whole

connotation: what is suggested by the word, in addition to the denotative or explicitly defined meaning

context processor: the neural networks that bring background knowledge and discourse to bear as word meanings are processed

cumulative instruction: teaching that proceeds in additive steps, building on what was previously taught

*derivational suffix: a type of bound morpheme; a suffix that can change the part of speech of a root or base word to which it is added, such as *–ity, -ive, -ly*

direct instruction: the teacher defines and teaches a concept, guides children through its application, and arranges for extended guided practice until mastery is achieved

dyslexia: an impairment of reading accuracy and fluency attributable to an underlying phonological deficit

ELL: English Language Learner

explicit instruction: the teacher defines the concept or association the student is to learn, provides guided practice with feedback, provides additional independent practice, and checks to see if the concept was learned, retained and applied

expository text: factual text written to "put out" information

* Advanced concepts are indicated with an asterisk.

gradable antonyms: words that are on opposite ends of a continuum; their meaning is relative and depends on the perspective of the user

hierarchical networks: organizational systems in which items exist in categories ordered from high (superordinate) to low (subordinate)

idiom: a phrase or expression different from the literal meaning of the words; a regional or individual expression with a unique meaning

indirect vocabulary learning: the process of learning words through incidental and contextual exposures, rather than through direct and deliberate teaching

inflection: a type of bound morpheme; a grammatical ending that does not change the part of speech of a word but that marks its tense, number, or degree in English (such as *-ed, -s, -ing*)

integrated: when lesson components are interwoven and flow smoothly together

*lexicon: name for the mental dictionary in every person's linguistic processing system

long-term memory: the memory system that stores information beyond 24 hours

Matthew Effect: coined by Keith Stanovich; a reference to the Biblical passage that the "rich get richer and the poor get poorer," insofar as the pattern of language and reading skills development in individuals over time

meaning processor: the neural networks that attach meanings to words that have been heard or decoded

metacognition: the ability to reflect on and understand our own thought processes

*metalinguistic awareness: an acquired level of awareness of language structure and function that allows us to reflect on and consciously manipulate the language we use

metaphor: words with nonliteral meaning, often expressed by an implied comparison of one thing to another or an unusual assignment of attributes ("the walls have ears")

morpheme: the smallest meaningful unit of the language

morphology: the study of the meaningful units in the language and how they are combined in word formation

multisyllabic: having more than one syllable

---

* Advanced concepts are indicated with an asterisk.

narrative: text that tells about sequences of events, usually with the structure of a story, fiction or nonfiction; often contrasted with expository text that reports factual information and the relationships among ideas

orthographic processor: the neural networks responsible for perceiving, storing, and retrieving the letter sequences in words

orthography: a writing system for representing language

paraphrase: express the thoughts in a sentence with different words

phoneme: a speech sound that combines with others in a language system to make words

phoneme awareness (also, phonemic awareness): the conscious awareness that words are made up of segments of our own speech that are represented with letters in an alphabetic orthography

phonics: the study of the relationships between letters and the sounds they represent; also used as a descriptor for code-based instruction in reading, e.g., "the phonics approach" or "phonic reading"

phonological awareness: meta-linguistic awareness of all levels of the speech sound system, including word boundaries, stress patterns, syllables, onset-rime units, and phonemes; a more encompassing term than phoneme awareness

phonological processor: a neural network in the frontal and temporal areas of the brain, usually the left cerebral hemisphere, that is specialized for speech sound perception and memory

phonological working memory: the "on-line" memory system that holds speech in mind long enough to extract meaning from it, or that holds onto words during reading and writing; a function of the phonological processor

phonology: the rule system within a language by which phonemes can be sequenced and uttered to make words

phrase-cued reading: the act of reading phrases that have already been marked or designated by underlining, spacing, or arrangement on the page

*pragmatics: the system of rules and conventions for using language and related gestures in a social context

prefix: a morpheme that precedes a root and that contributes to or modifies the meaning of a word; a common linguistic unit in Latin-based words

reading fluency: the ability to read text with sufficient speed and accuracy to support deep comprehension

* Advanced concepts are indicated with an asterisk.

referent: a word that another word or words refers to, e.g., the referent for a pronoun is a noun

root: a bound morpheme, usually of Latin origin, that cannot stand alone but that is used to form a family of words with related meanings

scaffolding: providing extra structure or support that enables the learner to perform successfully

schwa: the "empty" vowel in an unaccented syllable, such as the last syllables of *circus* and *bagel*

semantics: the study of word and phrase meanings

semantic features: the specific aspects of meaning associated with a word and that distinguish that word

shallow word learning: partial or limited knowledge of word that may be constricted to one context or one meaning instead of several

sound-symbol correspondence: same as phoneme-grapheme correspondence; the rules and patterns by which letters and letter combinations represent speech sounds

structural analysis: the study of affixes, base words, and roots

suffix: a derivational morpheme added to a root or base that often changes the word's part of speech and that modifies its meaning

syllable: the unit of pronunciation that is organized around a vowel; it may or may not have consonants before or after the vowel

syntax: the rule system by which words can be ordered in sentences

vocabulary: the body of words known by the speaker of a language; receptive or listening vocabulary is the body of word meanings recognized in context, whereas expressive vocabulary is the body of word meanings known well enough that they can be used appropriately by the speaker of a language

vowel: one of a set of 15 vowel phonemes in English, not including vowel-r combinations; an open phoneme that is the nucleus of every syllable; classified by tongue position and height (high-low, front-back)

word recognition: the instant recognition of a whole word in print

* Advanced concepts are indicated with an asterisk.

Appendix A

Multiple Meanings

Appendix A: Multiple Meanings

"House"[3]

Spellings: hus, hows, hous, huus, houus, huse, huis

Origin: Old Teutonic (huso)

Relatives: German - haus, Swiss - hus, Dutch - huis

Meanings:

a) a building for human habitation (c. 1000, Beowulf)

b) the portion of a building occupied by one tenant or family (c. 1020)

c) a building for human occupation, for some purpose other than that of an ordinary dwelling, usually with a prefix: workhouse, poorhouse, brewhouse (c. 1552)

d) a place of worship (c. 1000)

e) a building for entertainment of travelers, an inn (c. 1550), "on the house" (c. 1889, Kansas City, MO)

f) a building for the keeping of cattle, birds, plants (1503)

g) a place of abode of a religious fraternity, a convent (c. 1375)

h) a college in a university (1536)

i) a boarding-house attached to and forming a portion of a public school (c. 1855)

j) the building in which a legislative or deliberative assembly meets, or the assembly itself (1545)

k) a place of business, as in clearing-house, counting-house (1582), house of ill-fame (1810)

l) a theatre or playhouse

m) attribution of a permanent or resident band or jazz group (1934)

n) the persons living in one household (c. 950)

o) a family including ancestors and descendants (c.1000)

p) astrology—a twelfth part of the heavens as divided by great circles through the north and south points of the horizon (c. 1391, Chaucer)

q) phrases: house of ill repute, house of call, house and home, house-to-house, bring down the house, keep house, set up house, like a house on fire

[3] Listings based on entries for the word in J.A. Simpson (Ed.) (1989). *The Oxford English Dictionary*, 2nd Edition, Volume VII. Oxford: Oxford University Press.

    r)   special combinations: house boy, house arrest, house-bound, house call, house manager, house officer, house physician

    s)   compounds: housekeeper, householder, housebreaking

"Habitat"

Origin: Latin, habitat, habitare

Spelling: no change

Meaning:

    a)   the locality in which a plant or animal naturally grows and lives (c. 1762)

    b)   dwelling-place (c. 1854)

Combinations: habitat form, habitat group, Habitat for Humanity

Relatives: inhabit, cohabit

"Habitation"

Origin: Latin to French to English, abitacioun (habitation, c. 1374, Chaucer)

Meanings:

    a)   the action of dwelling in, occupy by inhabitants

    b)   a place of abode or residence, dwelling-place (1382)

    c)   a settlement

Relatives: cohabitation

"Residence"

Origin: Old French, Latin (residere)
    (1386, Chaucer)

Meanings:

    a)   having one's usual abode at a certain place

    b)   where a couple settles after marriage

    c)   living regularly at some place for the discharge of special duties

    d)   continuance in some course or action

    e)   the place where one resides

    f)   a dwelling, abode, or house

    g)   the seat of power

    h)   the time during which one resides at a place

    i)   the settling of sediment in liquids

Relatives: preside, president, presidential

Appendix B

Graphic Organizers

On the following pages are examples of graphic organizers that can be used before and after reading.

Graphic organizers used by permission from J. Greene, N. Eberhardt, A. Whitney, and L. Moats (2000). *LANGUAGE ! Curriculum, Instructional Resource Guide for Teachers*. Longmont, Colorado: Sopris West.

∿∿∿ Multiple Meaning Map ∿∿∿

Unit: _____   Student: _____   Date: _____

Directions: Use discussion with classmates, a thesaurus, or a dictionary to find multiple meanings for the word that is provided. Write a word or phrase to describe the word's meaning, or draw a picture to represent the meaning. Write a sentence using the word with each of the meanings.

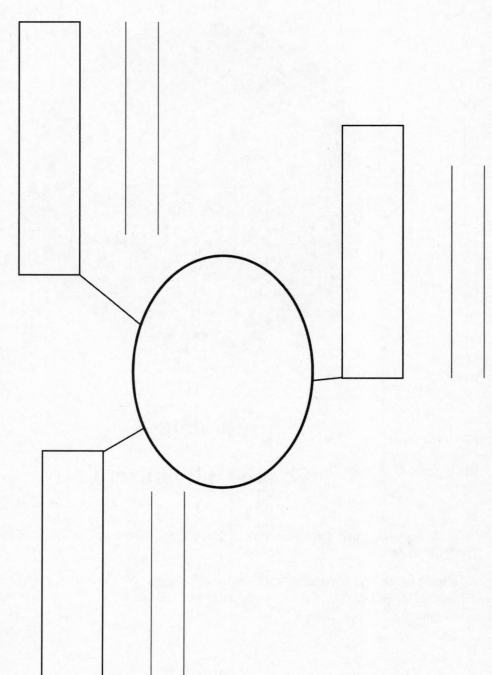

~~~ Map It: Classification Paragraph ~~~

Unit: _____   Student: _____   Date: _____

Category
_____

Subgroup
_____

Subgroup
_____

Subgroup
_____

(Examples)   (Examples)   (Examples)

～～～ **Relate It: Word Wheel** ～～～

Unit: _____ Student: _____ Date: _____

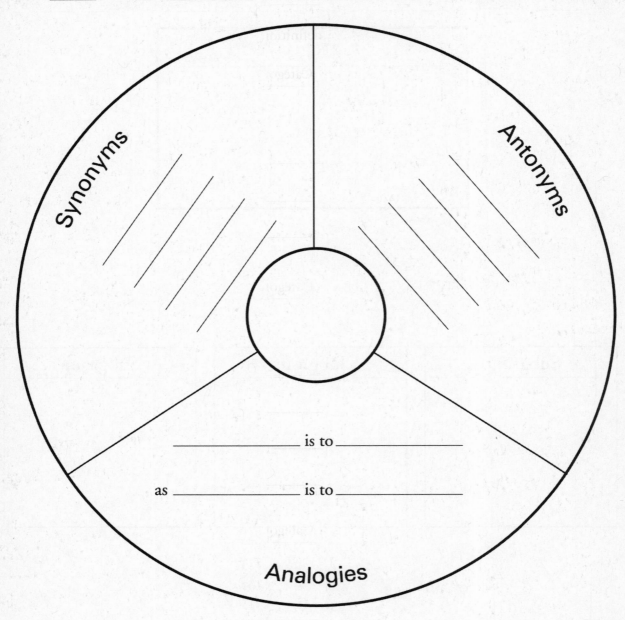

Write a sentence to show one of these relationships to the target word:

_____

_____

_____

～～～ Define It (Sheet A) ～～～

Unit: _____   Student: _____   Date: _____

Directions: Use this graphic organizer to build definitions for words in this unit.

1.

Word		Category		Attribute
	=		+	

Definition: _____

_____

2.

Word		Category		Attribute
	=		+	

Definition: _____

_____

_____

3.

Word		Category		Attribute
	=		+	

Definition: _____

_____

~~~~ **Define It (Sheet B)** ~~~~

Unit: _____ Student: _____ Date: _____

Directions: Use this graphic organizer to build an understanding of this word.

Category

What is it?

Properties/Attributes

What is it like?

What are some examples?

Illustrations/Examples

Appendix C

Model Lessons

Appendix C: Model Lessons

Little Bear Lost
Vocabulary Instruction

Pre-selected Vocabulary for Direct Instruction

Content-Specific	Key Words For In-Depth Teaching
cradleboard	responsibility
buffalo	silence
Lakota	enemy
Pawnee, Crow	pestered
lodge	terror, terrified
village	sob, sobbing
prairie	search
prairie grass	
doeskin	

Similes

. . . as warm and brown as the leaves that fell when frost lay on the grass

. . . as hot as the lodge fire in winter

. . . strong enough to shake the whole earth like thunder and with hoofs as wide as a cradleboard

Metaphors

. . . Blue Cloud felt her heart sink.

. . . her heart jumped

. . . that made her heart freeze in fear

. . . to find a whole sea of huge, hairy beasts running

I. Introductory Activities Before Reading

Look at pictures that help depict content-specific vocabulary and introduce it first to paint the setting and context for the story. Discuss Lakota life in the days when Lakota Sioux lived on the prairie, relied on buffalo for food, clothing, and shelter, and traveled continually in pursuit of the hunt. Ask why babies would be put on a cradleboard and why it would be dangerous if they cried. Ask who the enemies of the Lakota might have been; have the students heard of other tribes by the name of Pawnee and Crow.

Elaborate the use and meaning of *responsibility*. Say that this is a story about how a young girl handles a responsibility that was a little too much for her. Use the word "responsibility" many times in introductory conversation with students about their responsibilities. Give an example from your own life about responsibility that may not be easy for you carry out, or about a challenging responsibility you were given as a child. Ask other children to contribute experiences of their own. Use related terms *responsible*, *responsibility*, *irresponsible*.

Ask if students have heard of *pestered*. Give a clue that it has to do with being a *pest*, or bugging someone else until you get what you want.

Explain what *sob* means—to cry uncontrollably because you are very upset about something.

II. During Reading

In addition to other comprehension questions (see Module 6), ask students to paraphrase or interpret the metaphors and similes as they are read aloud. Alternatively, as students read a paragraph with a metaphor, ask students to find the phrases that tell how frightened Blue Cloud is [her heart sank . . . ; her heart froze . . .].

III. After Reading, Vocabulary Consolidation Activities

a) Put words for *crying* on cards and ask students to arrange them according to degree of upset they convey:

> whimper, whine, shed a tear, cry, bawl, sob

b) Create new similes:

as hot as _____

as frightened as _____

as clever as _____

c) Answer each question "yes" or "no" and then explain "why":

Did Blue Cloud forget to be responsible?

Was Blue Cloud's mother responsible?

Were Blue Cloud's friends responsible when they wanted to continue racing horses?

Would it be good if the baby sobbed when Blue Cloud searched for it?

Did Blue Cloud's mother pester her to take the cradleboard?

d) Match the word to another that means almost the same thing:

pester	baby-carrier
enemy	someone who wants to hurt you
cradleboard	search
look all over for	bug someone over and over

e) Create new sentences that use two or three vocabulary words together.

f) Ask students to paraphrase [restate in their own words] sentences and paragraphs in which figurative language is used.

g) Write a personal narrative about taking responsibility—successfully or unsuccessfully.

Mansion for a Mollusk
Vocabulary Instruction Activities

Pre-selected Vocabulary for Thorough Instruction
mansion
mollusk
protect, protection, protected
prevent
secrete, secreting, secreted
sturdy
mantle
moist
flesh

I. Vocabulary Activities Before Reading

a) Introduce title and focus on *mansion* and *mollusk*

b) Discuss different kinds of human homes and functions, listing words such as castle, trophy home, bungalow, cabin

c) Tell what a mollusk is—a soft, squishy animal that can live on land or sea—and ask students what they might know about mollusks (if anything!).

d) Say that mollusks—and all animals—need *protection*. Site examples of the kinds of protection that our houses give us—protection from extremes of temperature, sun, bad weather, predators. What do they use for *protection* when they are out in a storm?

e) Pronounce and write down other key words coming up: prevent, secrete, sturdy, mantle, moist, flesh.

II. Vocabulary Activities During Reading

a) Follow along and underline new words as they are read.

b) Or, put a post-it note where there is a new word they want to know more about. Can go back later and write definition on the post-it, then enter the word on a new words list.

c) Confirm a new meaning with the whole class as a word is read in context and discussed.

III. Vocabulary Activities After Reading

a) Rewrite phrases with the new words learned, or complete sentences with the new words. [protect, prevent, secrete, mantle, flesh]

1. The pads on a dog's foot _____ it from the rough ground and _____ it from getting sore.

2. The inside of the nose _____ fluid to keep it moist.

3. An outside cover over the skin is called a _____.

4. People, animals, and all warm-blooded things have _____ on their bones.

b) Have students combine two or more words into one sentence that shows the meaning of each. Have them work in partners so that everyone participates and may be called on to share.

> A mollusk seeks *shelter* to *protect* it from enemies.
> *Fleshy* slugs stay under rocks to keep *moist*.

c) Complete the semantic feature analysis chart:

	Soft	Fleshy	On land	In sea	Shell	No shell	Fixed to one place	Can move fast	Slow moving
whelk									
abalone									
squid									
octopus									
pearl oyster									
conch									
mussel									
snail									
slug									

d) Sort into categories all the mollusks named in the article:

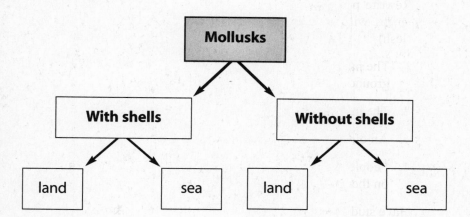

_____

_____

_____

_____

_____

_____

_____

_____

_____

_____

_____

_____

_____

_____

_____

_____

_____

_____

_____

_____

_____

_____

_____

_____

_____

_____

_____

_____

Appendix D

Text Resources for Teacher Exercises

Appendix D: Text Resources for Teacher Exercises

A Home for Lizzie

by Beth Thompson • Art by Noela Young

I was in the backyard pretending I was a goldminer and searching for treasure when I saw Lizzie. She was sitting on a rock, not moving at all. She could have been a leaf or a twig, because her nubbly skin blended in with the dark gray stone. But she was watching me. Then she slowly blinked her shiny, black eyes. It was like saying hello.

I named her Lizzie. When I said her name out loud, she lifted herself up on her tiny toes as if she were going to tiptoe away. But she didn't go. I guess she liked her name.

I think Lizzie knew I didn't want to hurt her. When I touched her back, she twitched her long, skinny tail. Maybe she thought my finger was a strange, new bug!

The sun had warmed Lizzie's rock. Now the rock felt like the back steps under bare toes. "Does that feel good to your toes, too?" I asked her. But Lizzie only blinked a blink that could mean "yes" . . . or could mean "no." And I don't know lizard language.

I found an empty butter tub under the kitchen sink. It was smooth and white and just the right size for a lizard home. It had a plastic almost-see-through lid. Mom helped me punch holes in the lid. I made six holes, so Lizzie would get lots of air.

I picked a handful of grass and sprinkled it inside the tub. Then I showed it to Lizzie.

"Look, your very own room," I told her. "You don't have to share." She blinked. "It has air conditioning. And a nice green rug you can nibble on. Do you like it?" Lizzie blinked "yes" . . . but it might have been "no."

I set her carefully on the grass in the tub. Then I put on the lid. I peeked through the holes to see what she would do.

Lizzie didn't move at first. Then she tried to climb up the side of the butter tub, but it was too smooth. She slid back to the grass and sat very still. She couldn't hide against the white plastic or the green grass. She couldn't warm herself against the cold, smooth tub. She couldn't feel the sun through the plastic ceiling of her new home.

I took off the lid and held it over my head, pretending I was Lizzie. Six tiny bits of sun shone through a cloudy window that needed washing. The wilted grass felt limp and coarse. Then I sniffed the tub. It smelled like butter and plastic and soap-under-the-sink, not at all like the backyard.

So I took Lizzie out of the butter tub and put her back on the rock. She didn't make a sound or run away. She just sat there, blinking. But I knew this time she meant "yes," because now Lizzie was home.

LITTLE BEAR LOST

BY MARY KAY MOREL

BEFORE HER BROTHER was born, Blue Cloud had only a doll to play with. The doll, plump with buffalo-hair stuffing, wore a finely beaded dress stitched by Blue Cloud's grandmother.

But the first time Blue Cloud laid eyes on her new baby brother, she forgot all about the doll. The baby looked as warm and brown as the leaves that fell when frost lay on the grass.

When Little Bear started to cry, his mother gently pinched his nose as all good Lakota mothers did. "A new one's first lesson must be silence," she explained.

Grandmother nodded. "The cry of a Lakota baby can warn an enemy who might be looking for our camp."

Blue Cloud shivered at the thought of any Crow or Pawnee warrior who might be hiding in the willow brush near her people's village. Then she looked at her baby brother again and forgot her fears.

"May I hold him?" Blue Cloud asked.

Her mother nodded. Blue Cloud carefully lifted the baby. He was heavier than her doll, and soon her arms began to ache.

As Little Bear grew, he spent most of his time in a cradleboard. Riding on his mother's back, he was safe from harm's way. But Blue Cloud longed to carry him. She pestered her poor mother to let her hold the baby almost every day.

One afternoon Blue Cloud's mother looked especially tired. The air was as hot as the lodge fire in winter. The

Art by Bradley Clark
© 2002 by Mary Kay Morel

sun beat hard on the buffalo grass as the Lakota people traveled the prairie in search of a new campsite.

"Please, Mother," Blue Cloud pleaded, "let Little Bear's cradleboard ride with me on my pony."

Her mother sighed wearily. "Perhaps this would be a good time for you to learn to care for your brother. But look after him well."

Blue Cloud felt very proud and grown-up carrying the cradleboard slung on the side of her slow-moving pony. She secretly smiled when other girls gathered around her on their horses, admiring Little Bear. Soon Blue Cloud was receiving so much attention that she and her friends lagged behind the moving village.

"Look!" Blue Cloud suddenly said in surprise. "Our people are a long way from us."

Why don't we race to them and see who has the fastest pony?" Little Hawk suggested.

All the girls were excited at the idea of a horse race. They were ready to start when Blue Cloud suddenly remembered Little Bear. "I can't race with my brother on my horse!" she cried.

Lay him in the grass," Little Hawk suggested. "We'll only race a short distance."

Blue Cloud looked down at her sleeping brother. A large rock stood nearby. Would it really hurt to leave him resting there for a short time? Climbing down from her pony, she gently laid his cradleboard against the stone.

"Come on!" Little Hawk shouted.

Blue Cloud leaped back onto her pony. In a flash, they were off, girls in doeskin racing across the prairie, their horses kicking a cloud of dust into the air.

The race was short. When it was over, two girls squabbled over who had won.

"Let's run another," one suggested.

Again and again they raced. Blue Cloud felt proud when she won the third race. But suddenly she remembered

Little Bear. "My brother!" Blue Cloud cried, whipping her horse around. "I must find him."

Looking back on the sea of buffalo grass, Blue Cloud felt her heart sink. Where was Little Bear? Where was the rock she had rested the cradleboard against?

Quickly, she began the search. When Blue Cloud saw the dusty tracks of a coyote, her heart jumped. What if her brother was in danger?

Kicking the pony's ribs, she hurried faster. Soon Blue Cloud spotted the dusty trail of a rattlesnake. What if Little Bear had been bitten? Blue Cloud felt tears sting her eyes at the thought of something so terrible happening to her brother.

If only Little Bear would make a sound! But Blue Cloud knew that Lakota babies were taught never to cry.

Then she saw something that made her heart freeze in fear. A thin brown line far away on the horizon was moving toward her

Buffalo! A whole herd!

Blue Cloud's hands shook as she held her pony's rope. She slowed her horse to a walk and leaned forward, watching in terror. What if the buffalo reached Little Bear before she did? What if her sleeping brother woke from his nap to find a whole sea of huge, hairy beasts running straight toward him? Beasts strong enough to shake the earth like thunder and with hoofs as wide as a cradleboard?

A sob rose in Blue Cloud's throat. Suddenly she could not stop crying. For several moments she sat sobbing, not aware that the pony had stopped moving. Then she heard the thumping sound.

Blue Cloud looked down. Her pony's hoof was pawing against the side of a rock. Next to the rock lay Blue Cloud's brother, sleeping soundly in the shade where she had left him.

Blue Cloud's mother was terrified when she heard how Little Bear had nearly been lost. Her anger lasted for many moons. "It is not easy being a mother," she reminded her daughter time and time again. "A child is a great responsibility."

Blue Cloud could only nod and hang her head down in shame.

As time passed, Little Bear grew into a sturdy young boy. He loved chasing rabbits and listening to stories told before the lodge fire.

His favorite tale was the one his sister told of how he had been lost on the prairie. As lodge smoke rolled upward to meet the stars, Blue Cloud would shyly begin the tale. And in the years to come, even their mother could listen and laugh (a little, at least) with the rest of Little Bear's family.

How the Whale Got His Throat

by
Rudyard
Kipling

IN THE SEA, once upon a time, O my best Beloved, there was a Whale, and he ate fishes. He ate the starfish and the garfish, and the crab and the dab, and the plaice and the dace, and the skate and his mate, and the mackereel and the pickereel, and the really truly twirly-whirly eel. All the fishes he could find in all the sea, he ate with his mouth—so! Till at last there was only one small fish left in all the sea, and he was a small 'Stute Fish, and he swam a little behind the Whale's right ear, so as to be out of harm's way.

Then the Whale stood up on his tail and said, "I'm hungry."

And the small 'Stute Fish said in a small 'stute voice, "Noble and generous Cetacean, have you ever tasted Man?"

"No," said the Whale. "What is it like?"

"Nice," said the small 'Stute Fish. "Nice but nubbly."

"Then fetch me some," said the Whale, and he made the sea froth up with his tail.

"One at a time is enough," said the 'Stute Fish. "If you swim to latitutde Fifty North, longitude Forty West (that is Magic), you will find, sitting *on* a raft, *in* the middle of the sea, with

nothing on but a pair of blue canvas breeches, a pair of suspenders (you must *not* forget the suspenders, Best Beloved), and a jackknife, one shipwrecked Mariner, who, it is only fair to tell you, is a man of infinite resource and sagacity."

So the Whale swam and swam to latitude Fifty North, longitude Forty West, as fast as he could swim, and *on* a raft, *in* the middle of the sea, *with* nothing to wear except a pair of blue canvas breeches, a pair of suspenders (you must particularly remember the suspenders, Best Beloved), *and* a jackknife, he found one single, solitary shipwrecked Mariner, trailing his toes in the water. (He had his mummy's leave to paddle, or else he would never have done it, because he was a man of infinite resource and sagacity.)

Then the Whale opened his mouth back and back and back till it nearly touched his tail, and he swallowed the shipwrecked Mariner, and the raft he was sitting on, and his blue canvas breeches, and the suspenders (which you *must* not forget), *and* the jackknife—he swallowed them all down into his warm, dark, inside cupboards, and then he smacked his lips—so— and turned round three times on his tail.

But as soon as the Mariner, who was a man of infinite resource and sagacity, found himself truly inside the Whale's warm, dark, inside cupboards, he stumped and he jumped and he thumped and he bumped, and he pranced and he danced, and he banged, and he clanged, and he hit and he bit, and he leaped and he creeped, and he prowled and he howled, and he hopped and he dropped, and he cried and he sighed, and he crawled and he bawled, and he stepped and he lepped, and he danced hornpipes where he shouldn't, and the Whale felt most unhappy indeed. (*Have* you forgotten the suspenders?)

So he said to the 'Stute Fish, "This man is very nubbly, and besides he is making me hiccup. What shall I do?"

"Tell him to come out," said the 'Stute Fish.

So the Whale called down his own throat to the shipwrecked Mariner, "Come out and behave yourself. I've got the hiccups."

"Nay, nay!" said the Mariner. "Not so, but far otherwise. Take me to my natal shore and the white cliffs of Albion, and I'll think about it." And he began to dance more than ever.

"You had better take him home," said the 'Stute Fish to the Whale. "I ought to have warned you that he is a man of infinite resource and sagacity."

So the Whale swam and swam and swam, with both flippers and his tail, as hard as he could for the hiccups; and at last he saw the Mariner's natal shore and the white cliffs of Albion, and he rushed halfway up the beach, and opened his mouth wide and wide and wide, and said, "Change here for Winchester, Ashuelot, Nashua, Keene, and stations on the *Fitch*burg Road"; and just as he said "Fitch" the Mariner walked out of his mouth. But while the Whale had been swimming, the Mariner, who was indeed a person of infinite resource and sagacity, had taken his jackknife and cut up the raft into a little square grating all running crisscross, and he had tied it firm with his suspenders (*now* you know why you were not to forget the suspenders!), and he dragged that grating good and tight into the Whale's throat, and there it stuck! Then he recited

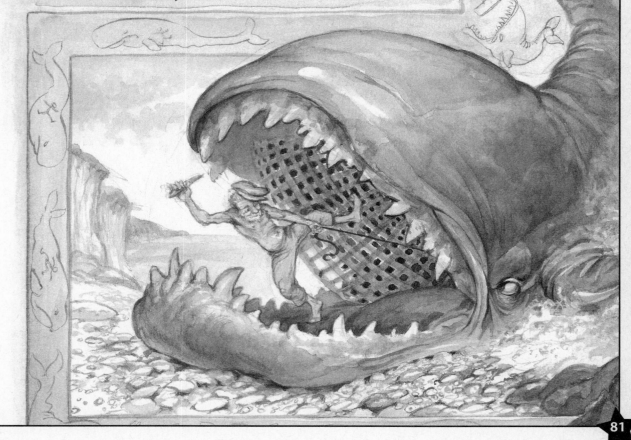

the following *sloka*, which, as you have not heard it, I will now proceed to relate:

> *By means of a grating*
> *I have stopped your ating.*

For the Mariner he was also a Hibernian. And he stepped out on the shingle and went home to his mother, who had given him leave to trail his toes in the water; and he married and lived happily ever afterward.

So did the Whale. But from that day on, the grating in his throat, which he could neither cough up nor swallow down, prevented him eating anything except very, very small fish; and that is the reason why whales nowadays never eat men or boys or little girls.

The small 'Stute Fish went and hid himself in the mud under the Doorsills of the Equator. He was afraid that the Whale might be angry with him.

The Sailor took the jackknife home. He was wearing the blue canvas breeches when he walked out on the shingle. The suspenders were left behind, you see, to tie the grating with; and that is the end of *that* tale.

Mansion for a Mollusk

by Catherine Ripley

Here's the challenge—you're an animal called a mollusk with a soft, squishy body. But, uh-oh, you don't have a ribcage to protect your heart the way a human does. And, uh-oh, you can't flash away from danger the way a fish does—unless you happen to be a special type of mollusk called a squid or an octopus. And, uh-oh, you don't have a lodge to shelter you the way a beaver does. So just how do you protect yourself? You grow yourself a house! And that's just what most mollusks do.

The Florida horse conch has a two-foot-long shell for protection. It is big and strong enough to eat other large sea snails in their shells.

[The original article showed a photograph of a Florida horse conch here.]

A Shell Is Like a House

The main job for the mollusk's
hard, sturdy home is to
protect the soft body inside.
This is especially true for
pearl oysters and mussels,
which fasten themselves
down and can't move. If
danger comes knocking, they
clam up tight as tight. Other
mollusks, such as conchs, abalones,
or whelks, carry their houses with
them as they slide around the ocean
bottom searching for food.

Like a house, a shell is also good protection
against the weather. This is especially important
for land mollusks. The shells of garden snails

[The original article showed a photograph of blue mussels here.]

Blue mussels can't move—so they snap shut when trouble comes!

This whelk travels on one big foot, which it also uses to pry open the shells of other mollusks, which it eats.

[The original article showed a photograph of a whelk here.]

Right-Handed or Left?

[The original article showed a photograph of a snail here.]

A snail shell is like a spiral staircase. The spirals go downward around a center pole to the opening at the bottom. For snails, the spirals get bigger and wider with each coil.

Snail shells can be right-handed or left-handed. Starting from the point, follow the coils downward. If they turn to the right, the shell is right-handed.

X-ray of a right-handed snail shell

prevent them from drying out. Land slugs, however, which are also mollusks, don't have shells. During hot or dry weather, many die because they can't keep their bodies moist.

[The original article showed a photograph of a spotted slug here.]

Without a shell, this spotted slug needs wet, dark places to stay all slimy—and alive!

Growing a Home from the Inside Out

All mollusks start out tiny—smaller than your baby fingernail—and all mollusks have a mantle, which is a layer of flesh surrounding the body. This mantle produces a shell partly by secreting a material called calcium carbonate, which the mollusk gets from its blood, the water around it, and even the food it eats. (Calcium carbonate also makes up eggshells.) Mollusks keep building their shells their whole lives. Once a mollusk reaches full size, the shell just gets thicker and thicker. Knock, knock! Anybody home?

[The original article showed a photograph of a blue mantle here.]

The blue mantle of a giant clam. Say ahh!

Animals Sharing Homes

Most wild animals live alone or with other animals like themselves. Some live out in the open. Others build nests or dig burrows. But not all animals build their own nests or dig their own burrows. And sometimes, two entirely different species of animals share a home!

[The original article showed a photograph of rhinos here.]

Red-billed oxpeckers eat, sleep, sunbathe, court, and mate on the backs of giant rhinos. Oxpeckers keep rhinos clean by eating ticks and flies found in their hides. In exchange for room and board, the birds warn the nearsighted rhinos of danger, by hopping and screeching and flapping their wings— even pecking the rhinos' heads if necessary!

When the European hermit crab grows, it moves into a new shell. It also looks for a sea anemone to attach to the shell. The anemone protects the crab by scaring away predators. And the crab gives the anemone a free ride to places where food is available.

[The original article showed a photograph of a hermit crab here.]

In hot, dry sandhills in Florida, the gopher tortoise digs a nice, cool burrow. But it doesn't live there alone! Snakes, gopher frogs, mice, and insects share the tortoise's home year-round. Armadillos, raccoons, foxes, and opossums drop in to find food, raise their young, or escape the grass fires that frequently rage across the sandhills.

[The original article showed a photograph of a gopher tortoise here.]

Language Essentials
for Teachers of
Reading and
Spelling

Appendix E

Answers to Applicable Exercises

Exercise #1: How We Learn Words

Think of a word you have learned recently. What was the context for that learning? What motivated you to learn and remember that word?

In the discussion, these points should arise: word learning occurs for a variety of reasons, including curiosity alone, the need to comprehend a passage, or the need to communicate with someone around a shared experience. Most people have to hear or read a word several times before they try to incorporate it into their own speaking vocabulary.

Exercise #2: Exploring the Use of Words in Context

Work with a partner. Choose an important word that is specific to a hobby or area of special knowledge that you have—a "jargon" word that a layperson would not know. Make up several sentences that use the word. Can your partner figure out what the word means? Could he or she define the word on the basis of the contextual uses you gave? How close was the meaning your partner came up with? What are the advantages and limitations of context use in word definition?

Context can help to a greater or lesser extent depending on the amount of redundant information that the surrounding text gives about the word. Context can be misleading. Exposure to a single contextual use of a word may not be enough to get the meaning; several exposures are often more helpful for narrowing down the word's meanings.

Exercise #3: Multiple Meanings

How many meanings and uses can you think of for the following common words: frame, check, pitch. Take one word and list all the meanings you know without using a dictionary. Then, check the dictionary for others you may have missed.

Frame: frame a picture; build the skeleton of a house; frame an innocent person accused of a crime; a sheltered box for growing plants from seeds
Check: bill at a restaurant; winning move in chess; body blow in ice hockey; check mark on paper; explore or look into (check up on...)
Pitch: throw a baseball to the batter; the angle of incline; black tar; try to sell an object or idea

Exercise #4: Categories

Put the following words on cards and then sort them into categories and subcategories. What do you need to know to accomplish this task?

mushing	Bruno	bones	fur/hair
jobs	Lassie	sniffing	retriever
kibbles	greyhound	famous dogs	legs
dogs	Rin-Tin-Tin	leading	spaniel
milkbone	tail	food	Fido
searching	terrier	breeds	body parts

DOGS

jobs	body parts	breeds	famous dogs	food
mushing	tail	terrier	Bruno	kibbles
searching	bones	greyhound	Lassie	milkbone
sniffing	fur/hair	spaniel	RinTinTin	(bones)
leading	legs	retriever	Fido	

Which graphic organizer in Appendix B would be most suitable for showing these word relationships?

Organizer on page 54

Exercise #5: Structure of Definitions

Use the following format to make a definition for each word below.

A _____ is (a) _____ that (is, does) _____ .
(critical features)

Words to define:

River: A river is a long, flowing body of water that goes downhill and that gets its water from many tributaries in a watershed.

Phoneme: A phoneme is a single speech sound that combines with others to make words. Every language has its own inventory of phonemes. Phonemes may be consonants or vowels.

Bison: A bison is a buffalo, a large brown animal with woolly fur that lives on the grassy plains of the Western United States and that once ran wild in very large herds before the west was settled.

Exercise #6: Semantic Feature Analysis

If the object at the top of a column has the feature designated on the left, mark a (+). If the object does not have the feature, mark a (–). How extensively do these meanings overlap? Are the words synonyms or not?

	OBJECTS		
FEATURES	**cup**	**glass**	**mug**
Have a handle	+/–	–	+
Made from clay	+/–	–	+
Made from glass	...	+	–
Round shape	+	+	+
Taller than round	–	+	–
For hot liquid	+/–	–	+
For cold liquid	+/–	–	+
Made from paper	+/–	–	–
Used for wine	+/–	+	–

Exercise #7: How Groups of Words Are Alike

In what way are the following groups of nouns the same and different? In what ways do their semantic features overlap?

1. daughter, sister, niece   vs.   nun, waitress, actress

   Both groups are female; the first group are relatives.
   _____

2. rooster, bull, ram   vs.   hen, ewe, cow

   Both groups are farm animals; the first are male.
   _____

3. table, chair, pencil   vs.   water, cream, sand

   Both groups of objects are inanimate; the first group are solid
   and can be counted; the second are fluid and cannot be counted.

4. table, chair, pencil   vs.   faith, hope, charity

   Both groups are nouns; the first are concrete, the second abstract.

5. husband, brother, son   vs.   clerk, preacher, judge

   Both groups are people; the first are relatives, the second
   are professionals.

6. grandfather, mother, nephew   vs   brother, sister, cousin

   Both groups are relatives; the first are multiple generations,
   the second are the same generation.

Exercise #8: Antonym Pairs and Scaling

Check the antonym pairs as complementary (either/or) or gradable (opposite ends of a continuous scale).

	Complementary	Gradable
dead – alive	✓	
hot – cold		✓
above – below	✓	
fat – skinny		✓
married – single	✓	
fragrant – putrid		✓
angry – delighted		✓
hideous – gorgeous		✓
straight – bent	✓	
honest – devious		✓
winner – loser	✓	

Now take one of the *continuous* antonym pairs and fill out the scale from one extreme to the other with words that show degrees of meaning.

←———— honest   straight   fair   dishonest   devious ————→

Exercise #9: Apply Strategies to Teaching Text

Focusing on one or more texts at the end of this module, work with a small group to a) select the words that you would teach directly and b) devise strategies for teaching those words. Indicate whether you are likely to use the strategies before reading, during reading, or after reading.

This exercise can take an hour or more. Select a text that is appropriate
for the group. The text on Animal Homes or the narrative, Little Bear
Lost are excellent selections for this exercise. Give the groups 20 to 30
minutes to sketch out their instructional strategies for just the vocabu-
lary part of the lesson. Use groups of 4 to 6 people. Give each group an
overhead transparency or chart paper to support a brief presentation by
the group. There are no "right" answers. Each group's approach will vary
and the sharing will enrich everyone's knowledge of potentially productive
approaches.